awrence
urrell
elected
oems
lited by Peter Porter

Mark
Ford
Six
Children

Poetry

Mark
Ford
S

Durs
Grünbein
A es for
  kfast
  hael Hofmann

ugust
leinzahler
he Strange
Iours
ravelers
eep

Lachlan
Mackinnon
The Jupiter
Collisions

Poetry

Lachlan
Mackinnon
Small
Hours

Jamie
McKendrick
Crocodiles
& Obelisks

dwin
Auir
elected
oems

Bernard
O'Donoghue
Farmers
Cross

Bernard
O'Donoghue
Selected
Poems

Tom Paulin
Fivemiletown

tephen
pender
New
Collected
oems

Wallace
Stevens
Collected
Poems

Wallace
Stevens
Selected
Poems

Adam
Zagajewski
Selected
Poems

This diary belongs to

....

First published in 2014
by Faber & Faber
Bloomsbury House
74–77 Great Russell Street
London WC1B 3DA

Designed and typeset by Faber & Faber Ltd

Printed in China by C&C Offset Printing Co., Ltd

Clauses in the Banking and Financial Dealings Act allow the government
to alter dates at short notice

A CIP record for this book is available from the British Library

ISBN 978–0–571–31158–3 (green cover edition)
ISBN 978–0–571–31163–7 (yellow cover edition)

The colours of this year's diary are taken from the first edition
of Seamus Heaney's 2006 collection, *District and Circle*.

Faber & Faber

Poetry Diary 2015

JANUARY

M	T	W	T	F	S	S
29	30	31	1	2	3	4
5	6	7	8	9	10	11
12	13	14	15	16	17	18
19	20	21	22	23	24	25
26	27	28	29	30	31	1
2	3	4	5	6	7	8

FEBRUARY

M	T	W	T	F	S	S
26	27	28	29	30	31	1
2	3	4	5	6	7	8
9	10	11	12	13	14	15
16	17	18	19	20	21	22
23	24	25	26	27	28	1
2	3	4	5	6	7	8

MARCH

M	T	W	T	F	S	S
23	24	25	26	27	28	1
2	3	4	5	6	7	8
9	10	11	12	13	14	15
16	17	18	19	20	21	22
23	24	25	26	27	28	29
30	31	1	2	3	4	5

APRIL

M	T	W	T	F	S	S
30	31	1	2	3	4	5
6	7	8	9	10	11	12
13	14	15	16	17	18	19
20	21	22	23	24	25	26
27	28	29	30	1	2	3
4	5	6	7	8	9	10

MAY

M	T	W	T	F	S	S
27	28	29	30	1	2	3
4	5	6	7	8	9	10
11	12	13	14	15	16	17
18	19	20	21	22	23	24
25	26	27	28	29	30	31
1	2	3	4	5	6	7

JUNE

M	T	W	T	F	S	S
1	2	3	4	5	6	7
8	9	10	11	12	13	14
15	16	17	18	19	20	21
22	23	24	25	26	27	28
29	30	1	2	3	4	5
6	7	8	9	10	11	12

JULY

M	T	W	T	F	S	S
29	30	1	2	3	4	5
6	7	8	9	10	11	12
13	14	15	16	17	18	19
20	21	22	23	24	25	26
27	28	29	30	31	1	2
3	4	5	6	7	8	9

AUGUST

M	T	W	T	F	S	S
27	28	29	30	31	1	2
3	4	5	6	7	8	9
10	11	12	13	14	15	16
17	18	19	20	21	22	23
24	25	26	27	28	29	30
31	1	2	3	4	5	6

SEPTEMBER

M	T	W	T	F	S	S
31	1	2	3	4	5	6
7	8	9	10	11	12	13
14	15	16	17	18	19	20
21	22	23	24	25	26	27
28	29	30	1	2	3	4
5	6	7	8	9	10	11

OCTOBER

M	T	W	T	F	S	S
28	29	30	1	2	3	4
5	6	7	8	9	10	11
12	13	14	15	16	17	18
19	20	21	22	23	24	25
26	27	28	29	30	31	1
2	3	4	5	6	7	8

NOVEMBER

M	T	W	T	F	S	S
26	27	28	29	30	31	1
2	3	4	5	6	7	8
9	10	11	12	13	14	15
16	17	18	19	20	21	22
23	24	25	26	27	28	29
30	1	2	3	4	5	6

DECEMBER

M	T	W	T	F	S	S
30	1	2	3	4	5	6
7	8	9	10	11	12	13
14	15	16	17	18	19	20
21	22	23	24	25	26	27
28	29	30	31	1	2	3
4	5	6	7	8	9	10

2014

JANUARY

M	T	W	T	F	S	S
30	31	1	2	3	4	5
6	7	8	9	10	11	12
13	14	15	16	17	18	19
20	21	22	23	24	25	26
27	28	29	30	31	1	2
3	4	5	6	7	8	9

FEBRUARY

M	T	W	T	F	S	S
27	28	29	30	31	1	2
3	4	5	6	7	8	9
10	11	12	13	14	15	16
17	18	19	20	21	22	23
24	25	26	27	28	1	2
3	4	5	6	7	8	9

MARCH

M	T	W	T	F	S	S
24	25	26	27	28	1	2
3	4	5	6	7	8	9
10	11	12	13	14	15	16
17	18	19	20	21	22	23
24	25	26	27	28	29	30
31	1	2	3	4	5	6

APRIL

M	T	W	T	F	S	S
31	1	2	3	4	5	6
7	8	9	10	11	12	13
14	15	16	17	18	19	20
21	22	23	24	25	26	27
28	29	30	1	2	3	4
5	6	7	8	9	10	11

MAY

M	T	W	T	F	S	S
28	29	30	1	2	3	4
5	6	7	8	9	10	11
12	13	14	15	16	17	18
19	20	21	22	23	24	25
26	27	28	29	30	31	1
2	3	4	5	6	7	8

JUNE

M	T	W	T	F	S	S
26	27	28	29	30	31	1
2	3	4	5	6	7	8
9	10	11	12	13	14	15
16	17	18	19	20	21	22
23	24	25	26	27	28	29
30	1	2	3	4	5	6

JULY

M	T	W	T	F	S	S
30	1	2	3	4	5	6
7	8	9	10	11	12	13
14	15	16	17	18	19	20
21	22	23	24	25	26	27
28	29	30	31	1	2	3
4	5	6	7	8	9	10

AUGUST

M	T	W	T	F	S	S
28	29	30	31	1	2	3
4	5	6	7	8	9	10
11	12	13	14	15	16	17
18	19	20	21	22	23	24
25	26	27	28	29	30	31
1	2	3	4	5	6	7

SEPTEMBER

M	T	W	T	F	S	S
1	2	3	4	5	6	7
8	9	10	11	12	13	14
15	16	17	18	19	20	21
22	23	24	25	26	27	28
29	30	1	2	3	4	5

OCTOBER

M	T	W	T	F	S	S
29	30	1	2	3	4	5
6	7	8	9	10	11	12
13	14	15	16	17	18	19
20	21	22	23	24	25	26
27	28	29	30	31	1	2

NOVEMBER

M	T	W	T	F	S	S
27	28	29	30	31	1	2
3	4	5	6	7	8	9
10	11	12	13	14	15	16
17	18	19	20	21	22	23
24	25	26	27	28	29	30

DECEMBER

M	T	W	T	F	S	S
1	2	3	4	5	6	7
8	9	10	11	12	13	14
15	16	17	18	19	20	21
22	23	24	25	26	27	28
29	30	31	1	2	3	4

2016

JANUARY

M	T	W	T	F	S	S
28	29	30	31	1	2	3
4	5	6	7	8	9	10
11	12	13	14	15	16	17
18	19	20	21	22	23	24
25	26	27	28	29	30	31
1	2	3	4	5	6	7

FEBRUARY

M	T	W	T	F	S	S
25	26	27	28	29	30	31
1	2	3	4	5	6	7
8	9	10	11	12	13	14
15	16	17	18	19	20	21
22	23	24	25	26	27	28
29	1	2	3	4	5	6

MARCH

M	T	W	T	F	S	S
29	1	2	3	4	5	6
7	8	9	10	11	12	13
14	15	16	17	18	19	20
21	22	23	24	25	26	27
28	29	30	31	1	2	3
4	5	6	7	8	9	10

APRIL

M	T	W	T	F	S	S
28	29	30	31	1	2	3
4	5	6	7	8	9	10
11	12	13	14	15	16	17
18	19	20	21	22	23	24
25	26	27	28	29	30	1
2	3	4	5	6	7	8

MAY

M	T	W	T	F	S	S
25	26	27	28	29	30	1
2	3	4	5	6	7	8
9	10	11	12	13	14	15
16	17	18	19	20	21	22
23	24	25	26	27	28	29
30	31	1	2	3	4	5

JUNE

M	T	W	T	F	S	S
30	31	1	2	3	4	5
6	7	8	9	10	11	12
13	14	15	16	17	18	19
20	21	22	23	24	25	26
27	28	29	30	1	2	3
4	5	6	7	8	9	10

JULY

M	T	W	T	F	S	S
27	28	29	30	1	2	3
4	5	6	7	8	9	10
11	12	13	14	15	16	17
18	19	20	21	22	23	24
25	26	27	28	29	30	31
1	2	3	4	5	6	7

AUGUST

M	T	W	T	F	S	S
1	2	3	4	5	6	7
8	9	10	11	12	13	14
15	16	17	18	19	20	21
22	23	24	25	26	27	28
29	30	31	1	2	3	4
5	6	7	8	9	10	11

SEPTEMBER

M	T	W	T	F	S	S
29	30	31	1	2	3	4
5	6	7	8	9	10	11
12	13	14	15	16	17	18
19	20	21	22	23	24	25
26	27	28	29	30	1	2
3	4	5	6	7	8	9

OCTOBER

M	T	W	T	F	S	S
26	27	28	29	30	1	2
3	4	5	6	7	8	9
10	11	12	13	14	15	16
17	18	19	20	21	22	23
24	25	26	27	28	29	30
31	1	2	3	4	5	6

NOVEMBER

M	T	W	T	F	S	S
31	1	2	3	4	5	6
7	8	9	10	11	12	13
14	15	16	17	18	19	20
21	22	23	24	25	26	27
28	29	30	1	2	3	4
5	6	7	8	9	10	11

DECEMBER

M	T	W	T	F	S	S
28	29	30	1	2	3	4
5	6	7	8	9	10	11
12	13	14	15	16	17	18
19	20	21	22	23	24	25
26	27	28	29	30	31	1
2	3	4	5	6	7	8

WINTERING
OUT

SEAMUS
HEANEY

29 Monday

30 Tuesday

31 Wednesday NEW YEAR'S EVE

1 Thursday NEW YEAR'S DAY (UK, IRL, CA, AUS, ZA, NZ)

2 Friday NEW YEAR'S HOLIDAY (SCT) DAY AFTER NEW YEAR'S DAY (NZ)

3 Saturday

4 Sunday

Poetry

In Wells Cathedral there's this ancient clock,
three parts time machine, one part zodiac.
Every fifteen minutes, knights on horseback
circle and joust, and for six hundred years

the same poor sucker riding counterways
has copped it full in the face with a lance.
To one side, some weird looking guy in a frock
back-heels a bell. Thus the quarter is struck.

It's empty in here, mostly. There's no God
to speak of – some bishops have said as much –
and five quid buys a person a new watch.
But even at night with the great doors locked

chimes sing out, and the sap who was knocked dead
comes cornering home wearing a new head.

5 Monday

6 Tuesday

7 Wednesday

8 Thursday

9 Friday

10 Saturday

11 Sunday

Streetlamps

Then there was more night
than we knew what to do with,
so we went into the street,
which had been waiting for us
all that time,

or if not for us,
then for anyone to come
and understand its spaces
the way the lamps do in their
cones of gaze.

We walked between them –
veiled sisters leaning over
their patches of ordinary
and making the moths sparkle
with meaning –

till what we said was
strung out in the same rhythm,
sentences left for the lights
to look at, and, in between,
our dark steps.

12 Monday

13 Tuesday

14 Wednesday

15 Thursday

16 Friday

17 Saturday

18 Sunday

In My Craft or Sullen Art

In my craft or sullen art
Exercised in the still night
When only the moon rages
And the lovers lie abed
With all their griefs in their arms,
I labour by singing light
Not for ambition or bread
Or the strut and trade of charms
On the ivory stages
But for the common wages
Of their most secret heart.

Not for the proud man apart
From the raging moon I write
On these spindrift pages
Nor for the towering dead
With their nightingales and psalms
But for the lovers, their arms
Round the griefs of the ages,
Who pay no praise or wages
Nor heed my craft or art.

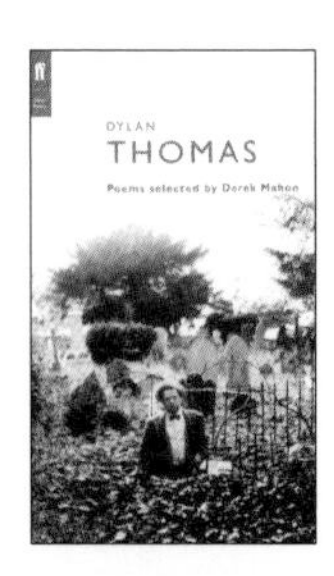

POET TO POET – *Dylan Thomas: Poems selected by Derek Mahon*

19 Monday

20 Tuesday

21 Wednesday

22 Thursday

23 Friday

24 Saturday

25 Sunday BURNS NIGHT

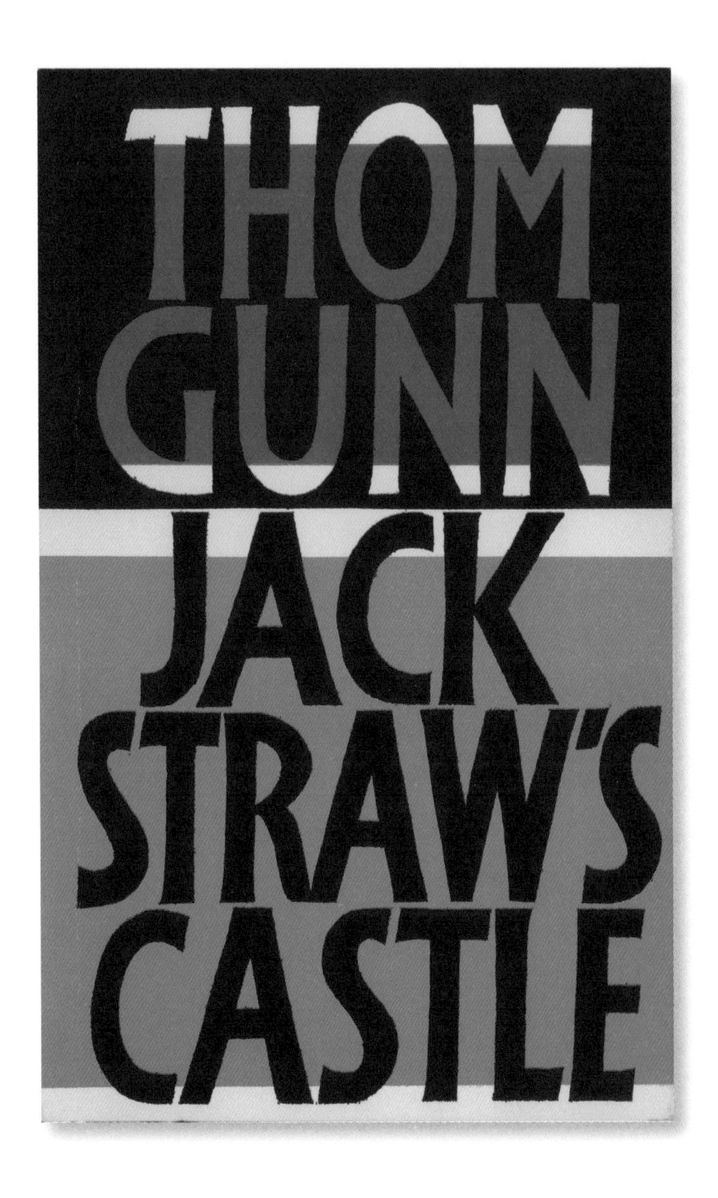
THOM
GUNN
JACK
STRAW'S
CASTLE

26 Monday AUSTRALIA DAY (AUS)

27 Tuesday

28 Wednesday

29 Thursday

30 Friday

31 Saturday

1 Sunday

After Africa

After Africa, Surbiton:
An unheated house, and flagstone pavements;
No colobus monkeys, no cheetahs scouring the plains.
Verrucas and weeping blisters ravaged our feet.

An unheated house, and flagstone pavements,
And snow falling through the halos of street lamps;
Verrucas and weeping blisters ravaged our feet;
But the shavings made by our carpenter, Chippy, were
as soft as bougainvillea flowers

Or snow falling through the halos of street lamps.
Everyone was pale, pale or grey, as pale or grey
As the shavings made by our carpenter, Chippy, which
were soft as bougainvillea flowers . . .
Red, African dust spilled from the wheels of our toy
trucks and cars.

Everyone was pale, pale or grey, as pale or grey
As the faded carpet on which
Red, African dust spilled from the wheels of our toy
trucks and cars.
Real traffic roared outside.

A faded carpet on which
Everything seemed after Africa; Surbiton's
Real traffic roared outside –
No colobus monkeys, no cheetahs scouring the plains.

2 Monday

3 Tuesday

4 Wednesday

5 Thursday

6 Friday WAITANGI DAY (NZ)

7 Saturday

8 Sunday

Espresso

Little cup of melancholy,
inch-deep well of the blackest
concentrate of brown,
it comes to your table without ceremony
and stands there shuddering
back to an inner repose.
Pinch it: it's still hot.

Soon, its mantle of bubbles
clears, but the eye –
all pupil, lustreless –
remains inscrutable.
Rightly so. This is your daily
communion with nothingness,
the nothingness within things.

Not to be sipped, it's a slug,
a jolt: one mouthful, then gone,
of comforting tarry harshness.
Which you carry now as a pledge
at the tongue's dead centre,
and the palate's, blessed
by both the swallowed moment
and its ghost, its stain.

9 Monday

10 Tuesday

11 Wednesday

12 Thursday

13 Friday

14 Saturday ST VALENTINE'S DAY

15 Sunday

Womans Constancy

Now thou hast lov'd me one whole day,
To morrow when thou leav'st, what wilt thou say?
Wilt thou then Antedate some new made vow?
        Or say that now
We are not just those persons, which we were?
Or, that oathes made in reverentiall feare
Of Love, and his wrath, any may forsweare?
Or, as true deaths, true maryages untie,
So lovers contracts, images of those,
Binde but till sleep, deaths image, them unloose?
        Or, your owne end to Justifie,
For having purpos'd change, and falsehood; you
Can have no way but falsehood to be true?
Vaine lunatique, against these scapes I could
        Dispute, and conquer, if I would,
        Which I abstaine to doe,
For by to morrow, I may thinke so too.

16 Monday

17 Tuesday SHROVE TUESDAY

18 Wednesday

19 Thursday

20 Friday

21 Saturday

22 Sunday

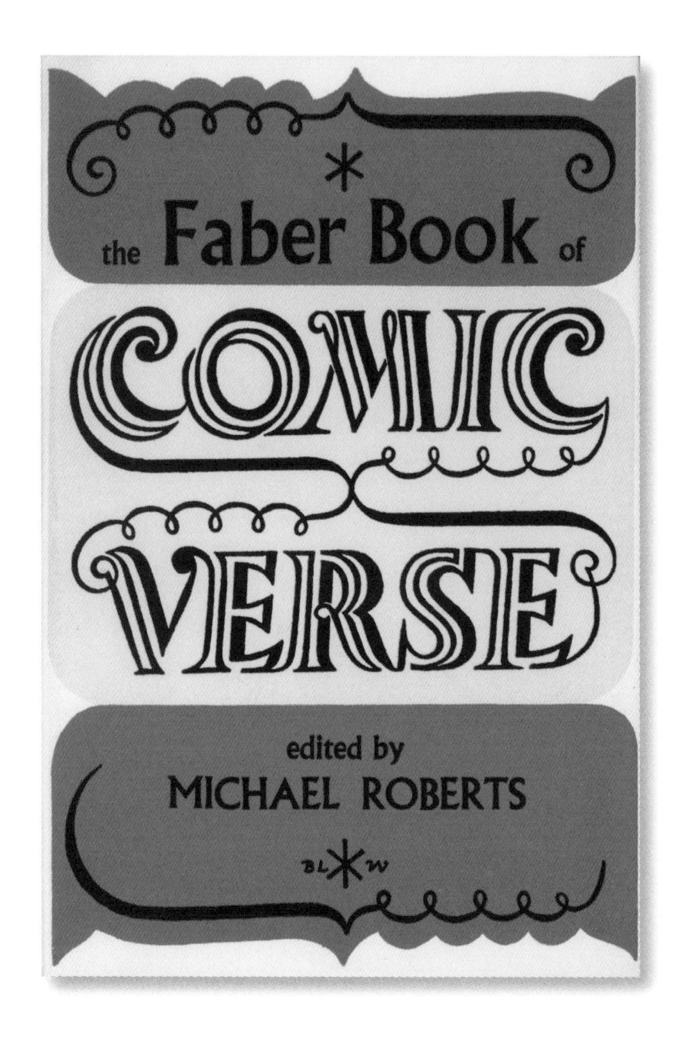
the Faber Book of
COMIC
VERSE
edited by
MICHAEL ROBERTS
BL W

23 Monday

24 Tuesday

25 Wednesday

26 Thursday

27 Friday

28 Saturday

1 Sunday ST DAVID'S DAY

Holy Island

I am behind you on the mainland, leaning
on your shoulder and pointing with one arm
in front of your face at weightless cinders
which are ravens blowing above the island.

Boulder clay on the outcrops, and beaches
dotted and dashed with coal dust. Guillemots
whitening the cliff face. Small orchids clearly
still evolving in a downpour of Arctic sunlight.

How many years are there left to cross over
and show you things themselves, not my idea
of things? Thirty, if I live to the age of my father.
I cannot explain why I have left it as late as this.

Your black hair blows into my eyes, and I see
everything moving fast now. Weather polishes
the silver fields ahead. The ravens swoop down
and settle in the gorgeous pages of the gospels.

2 Monday

3 Tuesday

4 Wednesday

5 Thursday

6 Friday

7 Saturday

8 Sunday

Mirror

I am silver and exact. I have no preconceptions.
Whatever I see I swallow immediately
Just as it is, unmisted by love or dislike.
I am not cruel, only truthful –
The eye of a little god, four-cornered.
Most of the time I meditate on the opposite wall.
It is pink, with speckles. I have looked at it so long
I think it is a part of my heart. But it flickers.
Faces and darkness separate us over and over.

Now I am a lake. A woman bends over me,
Searching my reaches for what she really is.
Then she turns to those liars, the candles or the moon.
I see her back, and reflect it faithfully.
She rewards me with tears and an agitation of hands.
I am important to her. She comes and goes.
Each morning it is her face that replaces the darkness.
In me she has drowned a young girl, and in me an old
    woman
Rises toward her day after day, like a terrible fish.

9 Monday

10 Tuesday

11 Wednesday

12 Thursday

13 Friday

14 Saturday

15 Sunday

On First Looking into Chapman's Homer

Much have I travelled in the realms of gold,
And many goodly states and kingdoms seen;
Round many western islands have I been
Which bards in fealty to Apollo hold.
Oft of one wide expanse had I been told
That deep-browed Homer rules as his demesne;
Yet did I never breathe its pure serene
Till I heard Chapman speak out loud and bold:
Then felt I like some watcher of the skies
When a new planet swims into his ken;
Or like stout Cortez when with eagle eyes
He stared at the Pacific – and all his men
Looked at each other with a wild surmise –
Silent, upon a peak in Darien.

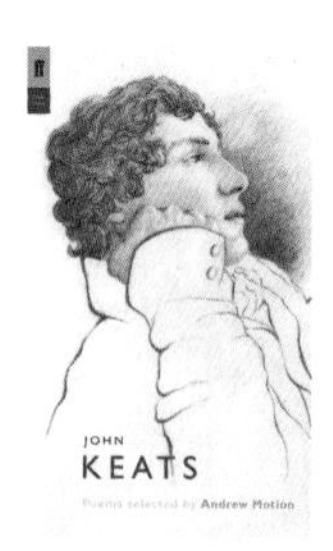

16 Monday

17 Tuesday ST PATRICK'S DAY (IRL, NI)

18 Wednesday

19 Thursday

20 Friday

21 Saturday HUMAN RIGHTS DAY (ZA) 22 Sunday

WODWO
TED
HUGHES

23 Monday

24 Tuesday

25 Wednesday

26 Thursday

27 Friday

28 Saturday

29 Sunday

Field

Easternight, the mind's midwinter

I stood in the big field behind the house
at the centre of all visible darkness

a brick of earth, a block of sky,
there lay the world, wedged
between its premise and its conclusion

some star let go a small sound on a thread.

almost midnight – I could feel the earth's
soaking darkness squeeze and fill its darkness,
everything spinning into the spasm of midnight

and for a moment, this high field unhorizoned
hung upon nothing, barking for its owner

burial, widowed, moonless, seeping

docks, grasses, small windflowers, weepholes, wires

30 Monday

31 Tuesday

1 Wednesday

2 Thursday

3 Friday GOOD FRIDAY (UK, IRL, CA, AUS, ZA, NZ)

4 Saturday EASTER SATURDAY (AUS) 5 Sunday EASTER SUNDAY (UK, AUS, ZA)

Preludes
IV

His soul stretched tight across the skies
That fade behind a city block,
Or trampled by insistent feet
At four and five and six o'clock;
And short square fingers stuffing pipes,
And evening newspapers, and eyes
Assured of certain certainties,
The conscience of a blackened street
Impatient to assume the world.

I am moved by fancies that are curled
Around these images, and cling:
The notion of some infinitely gentle
Infinitely suffering thing.

Wipe your hand across your mouth, and laugh;
The worlds revolve like ancient women
Gathering fuel in vacant lots.

6 Monday EASTER MONDAY (UK, IRL, CA, AUS, NZ) FAMILY DAY (ZA)

7 Tuesday

8 Wednesday

9 Thursday

10 Friday

11 Saturday

12 Sunday

Bumbarrel's Nest

The oddling bush, close sheltered hedge new-plashed,
Of which spring's early liking makes a guest
First with a shade of green though winter-dashed –
There, full as soon, bumbarrels make a nest
Of mosses grey with cobwebs closely tied
And warm and rich as feather-bed within,
With little hole on its contrary side
That pathway peepers may no knowledge win
Of what her little oval nest contains –
Ten eggs and often twelve, with dusts of red
Soft frittered – and full soon the little lanes
Screen the young crowd and hear the twitt'ring song
Of the old birds who call them to be fed
While down the hedge they hang and hide along.

13 Monday

14 Tuesday

15 Wednesday

16 Thursday

17 Friday

18 Saturday

19 Sunday

The Long Walk to the End of the Garden

The rusty stain on the pillow, the rumble of pain
in your knee, impromptus of a dream in which

you hacked your way out again and again, the dawn
fading up from the green-blue-green of the silver birch,

a flourish on the surface of the pond, a ragged skein
of bindweed on the stone-cold statuette

of that thin-lipped girl from the dream, the odds-on bet
that nothing returns or renews, that the stain

is just what it seems, that the sudden catch
in the throat, the moment of blind regret,

will be all in all, that your way through the garden wet
will take you, for sure, out by the willow-arch

on a morning much like this, and into the lane
beyond which must lie the far field, beyond which

a nameless road, beyond which a landline drawn
in clumsy charcoal below a clumsy sketch

of yourself as pseudocide, a frantic silhouette
soon smudged to shadow by incoming rain.

20 Monday

21 Tuesday

22 Wednesday

23 Thursday ST GEORGE'S DAY

24 Friday

25 Saturday ANZAC DAY (AUS, NZ) 26 Sunday

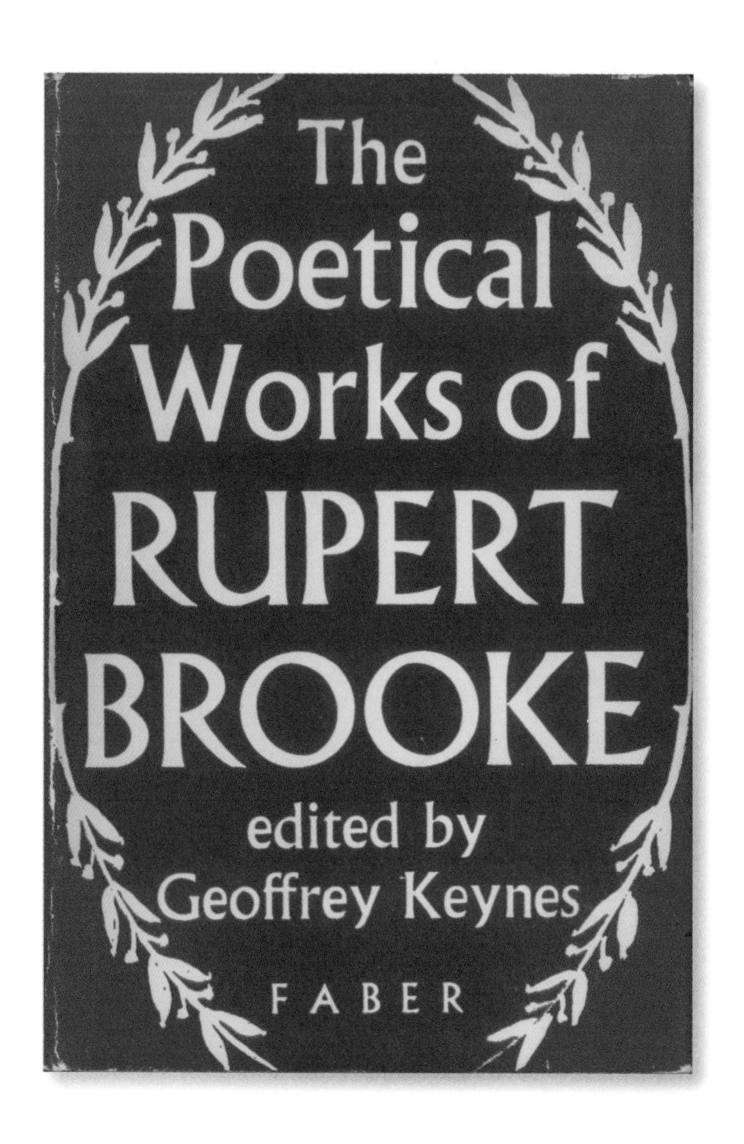
The
Poetical
Works of
RUPERT
BROOKE
edited by
Geoffrey Keynes
FABER

27 Monday FREEDOM DAY (ZA)

28 Tuesday

29 Wednesday

30 Thursday

1 Friday WORKERS' DAY (ZA)

2 Saturday

3 Sunday

The Sphinx

Did it once issue from the carver's hand
Healthy? Even the earliest conqueror saw
The face of a sick ape, a bandaged paw,
An ailing lion crouched on dirty sand.

We gape, the go uneasily away:
It does not like the young nor love nor learning.
Time hurt it like a person: it lies turning
A vast behind on shrill America,

And witnesses. The huge hurt face accuses
And pardons nothing, least of all success:
What counsel it might offer it refuses
To those who face akimbo its distress.

'Do people like me?' *No*. The slave amuses
The lion. 'Am I to suffer always?' *Yes*.

4 Monday EARLY MAY BANK HOLIDAY (UK) MAY DAY (IRL)

5 Tuesday

6 Wednesday

7 Thursday

8 Friday

9 Saturday

10 Sunday

Love after Love

The time will come
when, with elation,
you will greet yourself arriving
at your own door, in your own mirror,
and each will smile at the other's welcome,

and say, sit here. Eat.
You will love again the stranger who was your self.
Give wine. Give bread. Give back your heart
to itself, to the stranger who has loved you

all your life, whom you ignored
for another, who knows you by heart.
Take down the love letters from the bookshelf,

the photographs, the desperate notes,
peel your own image from the mirror.
Sit. Feast on your life.

11 Monday

12 Tuesday

13 Wednesday

14 Thursday

15 Friday

16 Saturday

17 Sunday

Silver

Slowly, silently, now the moon
Walks the night in her silver shoon;
This way, and that, she peers, and sees
Silver fruit upon silver trees;
One by one the casements catch
Her beams beneath the silvery thatch;
Couched in his kennel, like a log,
With paws of silver sleeps the dog;
From their shadowy cote the white breasts peep
Of doves in a silver-feathered sleep;
A harvest mouse goes scampering by,
With silver claws, and silver eye;
And moveless fish in the water gleam,
By silver reeds in a silver stream.

18 Monday VICTORIA DAY (CA)

19 Tuesday

20 Wednesday

21 Thursday

22 Friday

23 Saturday

24 Sunday

Epithalamium

You're beeswax and I'm birdshit.
I'm mostly harmless. You're irrational.
If I'm iniquity then you're theft.
One of us is supercalifragilistic.

If I'm the most insane disgusting filth
you're hardly curiosa.
You're bubblewrap to my fingertips.
You're winter sleep and I'm the bee dance.

And I am menthol and you are eggshell.
When you're atrocious I am Spellcheck.
You're the yen. I'm the Nepalese pound.
If I'm homesteading you're radical chic.

I'm carpet shock and you're the rail.
I'm Memory Foam Day on Price-Drop TV
and you're the Lord of Misrule who shrieks
when I surface in goggles through duckweed,

and I am Trafalgar, and you're Waterloo,
and frequently it seems to me that I am you,
and you are me. If I'm the rising incantation
you're the charm, or I am, or you are.

25 Monday SPRING BANK HOLIDAY (UK)

26 Tuesday

27 Wednesday

28 Thursday

29 Friday

30 Saturday

31 Sunday

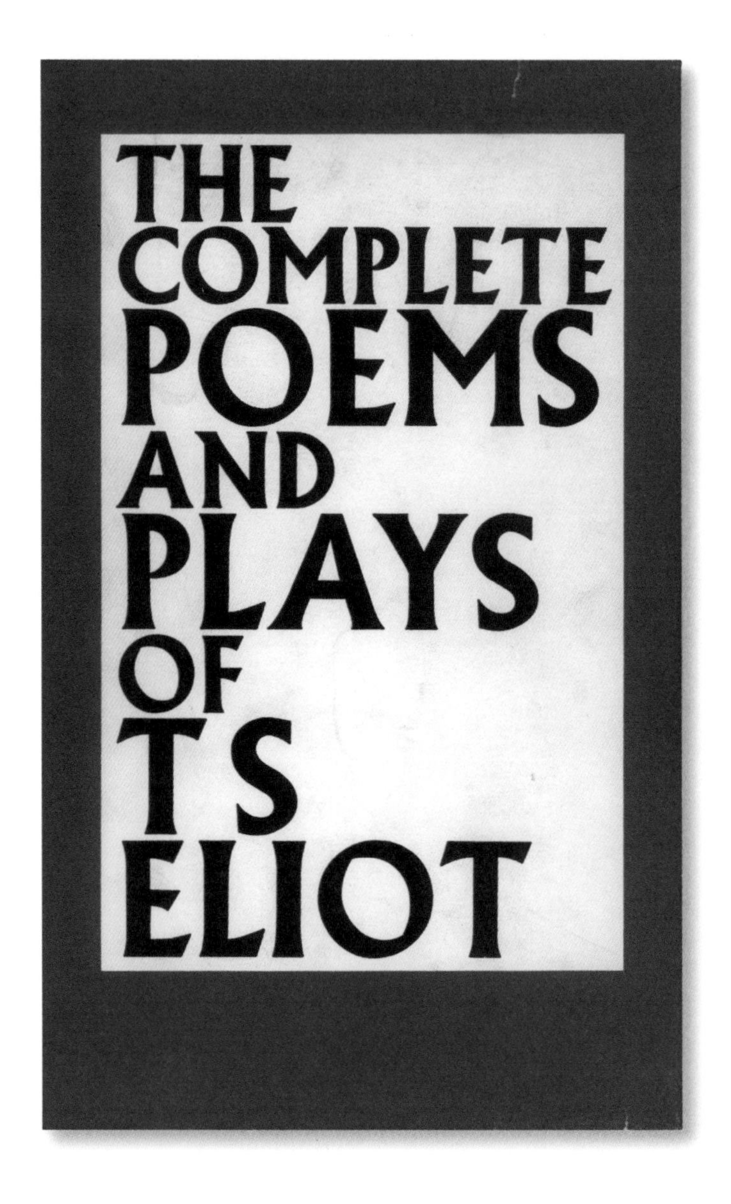
THE
COMPLETE
POEMS
AND
PLAYS
OF
T S
ELIOT

1 Monday JUNE BANK HOLIDAY (IRL) QUEEN'S BIRTHDAY HOLIDAY (NZ)

2 Tuesday

3 Wednesday

4 Thursday

5 Friday

6 Saturday

7 Sunday

To the Virgins, to Make Much of Time

Gather ye Rose-buds while ye may,
    Old Time is still a flying:
And this same flower that smiles to day,
    To morrow will be dying.

The glorious Lamp of Heaven, the Sun,
    The higher he's a getting;
The sooner will his Race be run,
    An neerer he's to Setting.

That Age is best, which is the first,
    When Youth and Blood are warmer;
But being spent, the worse, and worst
    Times, still succeed the former.

Then be not coy, but use your time;
    And while ye may, goe marry:
For having lost but once your prime,
    You may for ever tarry.

8 Monday

9 Tuesday

10 Wednesday

11 Thursday

12 Friday

13 Saturday

14 Sunday

Forget What Did

Stopping the diary
Was a stun to memory,
Was a blank starting,

One no longer cicatrized
By such words, such actions
As bleakened waking.

I wanted them over,
Hurried to burial
And looked back on

Like the wars and winters
Missing behind the windows
Of an opaque childhood.

And the empty pages?
Should they ever be filled
Let it be with observed

Celestial recurrences,
The day the flowers come,
And when the birds go.

15 Monday

16 Tuesday YOUTH DAY (ZA)

17 Wednesday

18 Thursday

19 Friday

20 Saturday

21 Sunday

Poetry

A version of Antonio Machado

In the same way that the mindless diamond keeps
one spark of the planet's early fires
trapped forever in its net of ice,
it's not love's later heat that poetry holds,
but the atom of the love that drew it forth
from the silence: so if the bright coal of his love
begins to smoulder, the poet hears his voice
suddenly forced, like a bar-room singer's – boastful
with his own huge feeling, or drowned by violins;
but if it yields a steadier light, he knows
the pure verse, when it finally comes, will sound
like a mountain spring, anonymous and serene.
Beneath the blue oblivious sky, the water
sings of nothing, not your name, not mine.

22 Monday

23 Tuesday

24 Wednesday

25 Thursday

26 Friday

27 Saturday

28 Sunday

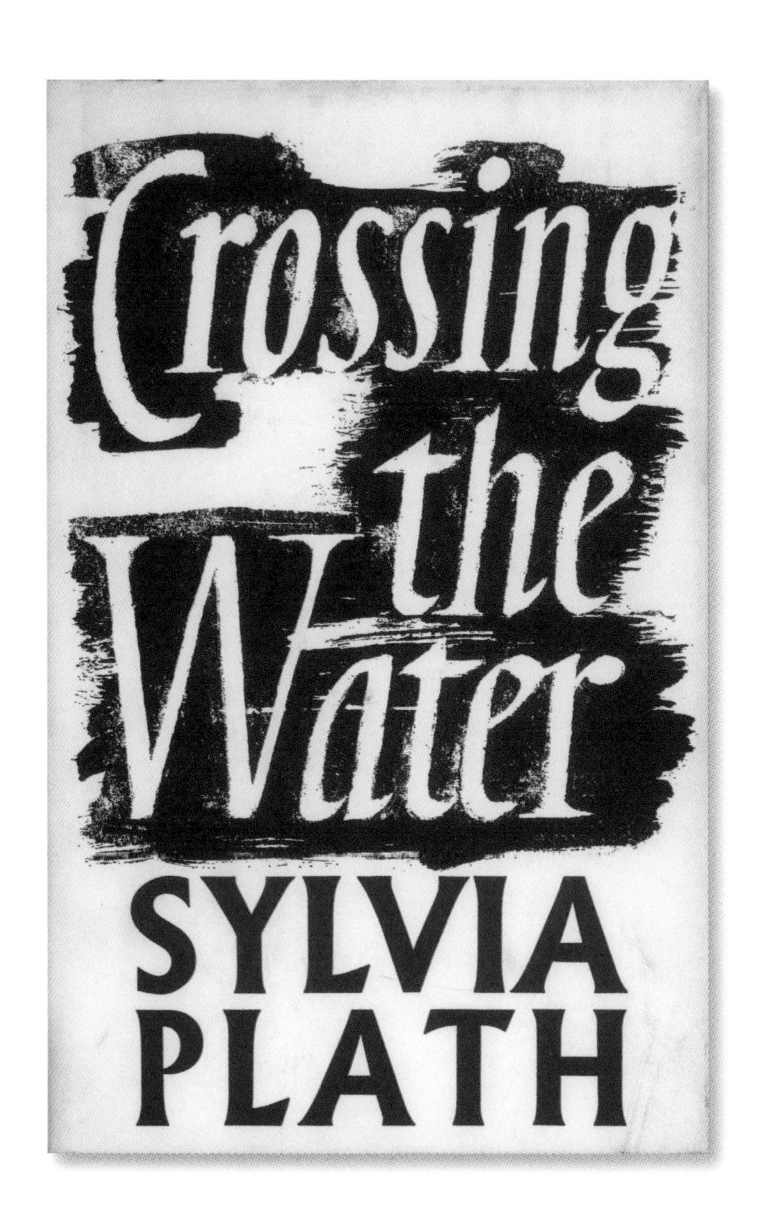
Crossing the Water
SYLVIA PLATH

29 Monday

30 Tuesday

1 Wednesday CANADA DAY (CA)

2 Thursday

3 Friday

4 Saturday

5 Sunday

The Crickets sang
And set the Sun
And Workmen finished one by one
Their Seam the Day upon.

The low Grass loaded with the Dew
The Twilight stood, as Strangers do
With Hat in Hand, polite and new
To stay as if, or go.

A Vastness, as a Neighbor, came,
A Wisdom, without Face, or Name,
A Peace, as Hemispheres at Home
And so the Night became.

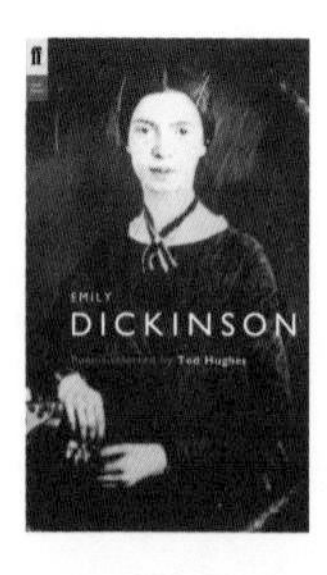

6 Monday

7 Tuesday

8 Wednesday

9 Thursday

10 Friday

11 Saturday

12 Sunday

Seferis

Time quietly compiling us like sheaves
Turns around one day, beckons the special few,
With one bird singing somewhere in the leaves,
Someone like K. or somebody like you,
Free-falling target for the envious thrust,
So tilting into darkness go we must.

Thus the fading writer signing off
Sees in the vast perspectives of dispersal
His words float off like tiny seeds,
Wind-borne or bird-distributed notes,
To the very end of loves without rehearsal,
The stinging image riper than his deeds.

Yours must have set out like ancient
Colonists, from Delos or from Rhodes,
To dare the sun-gods, found great entrepôts,
Naples or Rio, far from man's known abodes,
To confer the quaint Grecian script on other men;
A new Greek fire ignited by your pen.

How marvellous to have done it and then left
It in the lost property office of the loving mind,
The secret whisper those who listen find.
You show us all the way the great ones went,
In silences becalmed, so well they knew
That even to die is somehow to invent.

13 Monday BATTLE OF THE BOYNE HOLIDAY (NI)

14 Tuesday

15 Wednesday

16 Thursday

17 Friday

18 Saturday

19 Sunday

Window

His sadness was double,
it had two edges.

One looked out –
onto skylines,
and streets with ice-cream
men, and cars,
and clouds
like cut cotton.

The other stayed in
to watch
his memories unbuckle
and his hairs
all repeat
in the washstand.

Both were impatient.
Sometimes they'd meet
and make a window.

'Look at the world!' said the glass.
'Look at the glass!' said the world.

20 Monday

21 Tuesday

22 Wednesday

23 Thursday

24 Friday

25 Saturday

26 Sunday

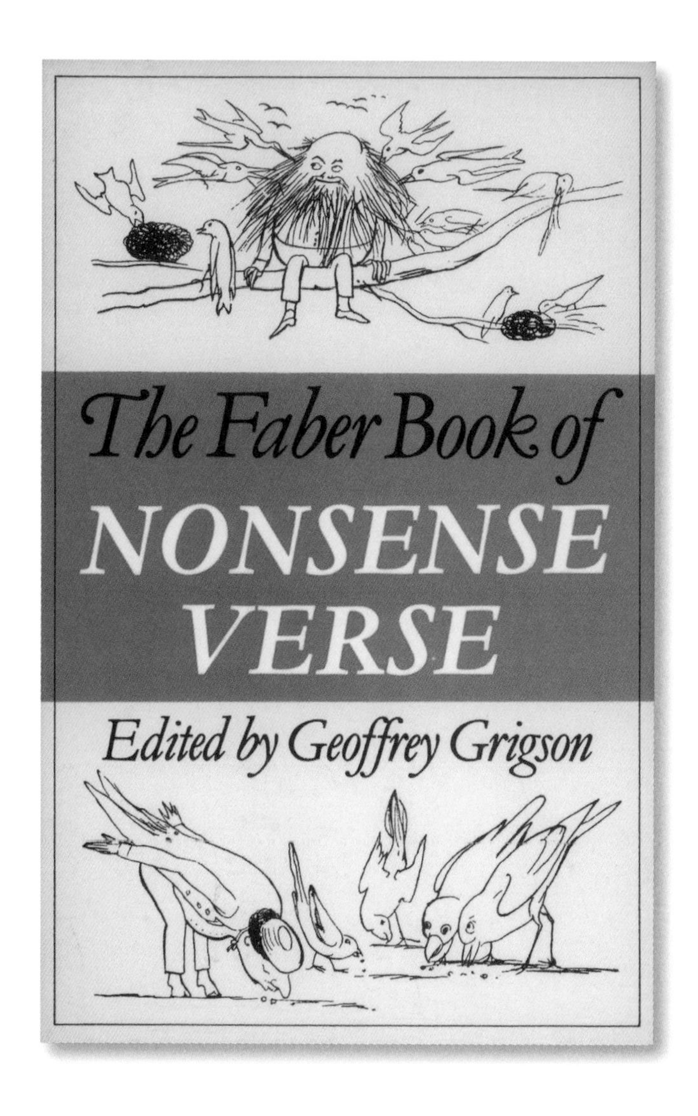
The Faber Book of
NONSENSE
VERSE
Edited by Geoffrey Grigson

27 Monday

28 Tuesday

29 Wednesday

30 Thursday

31 Friday

1 Saturday

2 Sunday

Coleridge

So great a storm I rose in the night,
my mind in the hills, a dream of lateness.
What was it in my countenance
that made them harness thirty horses?
When at last they pulled together
we travelled with such speed and force
the driver threw the reins aside:
'Everything that's for us is against us.
We're going nowhere tonight.'

3 Monday SUMMER BANK HOLIDAY (SCT, IRL)

4 Tuesday

5 Wednesday

6 Thursday

7 Friday

8 Saturday

9 Sunday

Sunday Morning Apples
To William Sommer

The leaves will fall again sometime and fill
The fleece of nature with those purposes
That are your rich and faithful strength of line.

But now there are challenges to spring
In that ripe nude with head,
reared
Into a realm of swords, her purple shadow
Bursting on the winter of the world
From whiteness that cries defiance to the snow.

A boy runs with a dog before the sun, straddling
Spontaneities that form their independent orbits,
Their own perennials of light
In the valley where you live
(called Brandywine).

I have seen the apples there that toss you secrets, –
Beloved apples of seasonable madness
That feed your inquiries with aerial wine.

Put them again beside a pitcher with a knife,
And poise them full and ready for explosion –
The apples, Bill, the apples!

10 Monday NATIONAL WOMEN'S DAY HOLIDAY (ZA)

11 Tuesday

12 Wednesday

13 Thursday

14 Friday

15 Saturday

16 Sunday

Over the Hills

Often and often it came back again
To mind, the day I passed the horizon ridge
To a new country, the path I had to find
By half-gaps that were stiles once in the hedge,
The pack of scarlet clouds running across
The harvest evening that seemed endless then
And after, and the inn where all were kind,
All were strangers. I did not know my loss
Till one day twelve months later suddenly
I leaned upon my spade and saw it all,
Though far beyond the sky-line. It became
Almost a habit through the year for me
To lean and see it and think to do the same
Again for two days and a night. Recall
Was vain: no more could the restless brook
Ever turn back and climb the waterfall
To the lake that rests and stirs not in its nook,
As in the hollow of the collar-bone
Under the mountain's head of rush and stone.

17 Monday

18 Tuesday

19 Wednesday

20 Thursday

21 Friday

22 Saturday

23 Sunday

The Licorice Fields at Pontefract

In the licorice fields at Pontefract
    My love and I did meet
And many a burdened licorice bush
    Was blooming round our feet;
Red hair she had and golden skin,
Her sulky lips were shaped for sin,
Her sturdy legs were flannel-slack'd,
The strongest legs in Pontefract.

The light and dangling licorice flowers
    Gave off the sweetest smells;
From various black Victorian towers
    The Sunday evening bells
Came pealing over dales and hills
And tanneries and silent mills
And lowly streets where country stops
And little shuttered corner shops.

She cast her blazing eyes on me
    And plucked a licorice leaf;
I was her captive slave and she
    My red-haired robber chief.
Oh love! for love I could not speak,
It left me winded, wilting, weak
And held in brown arms strong and bare
And wound with flaming ropes of hair.

24 Monday

25 Tuesday

26 Wednesday

27 Thursday

28 Friday

29 Saturday

30 Sunday

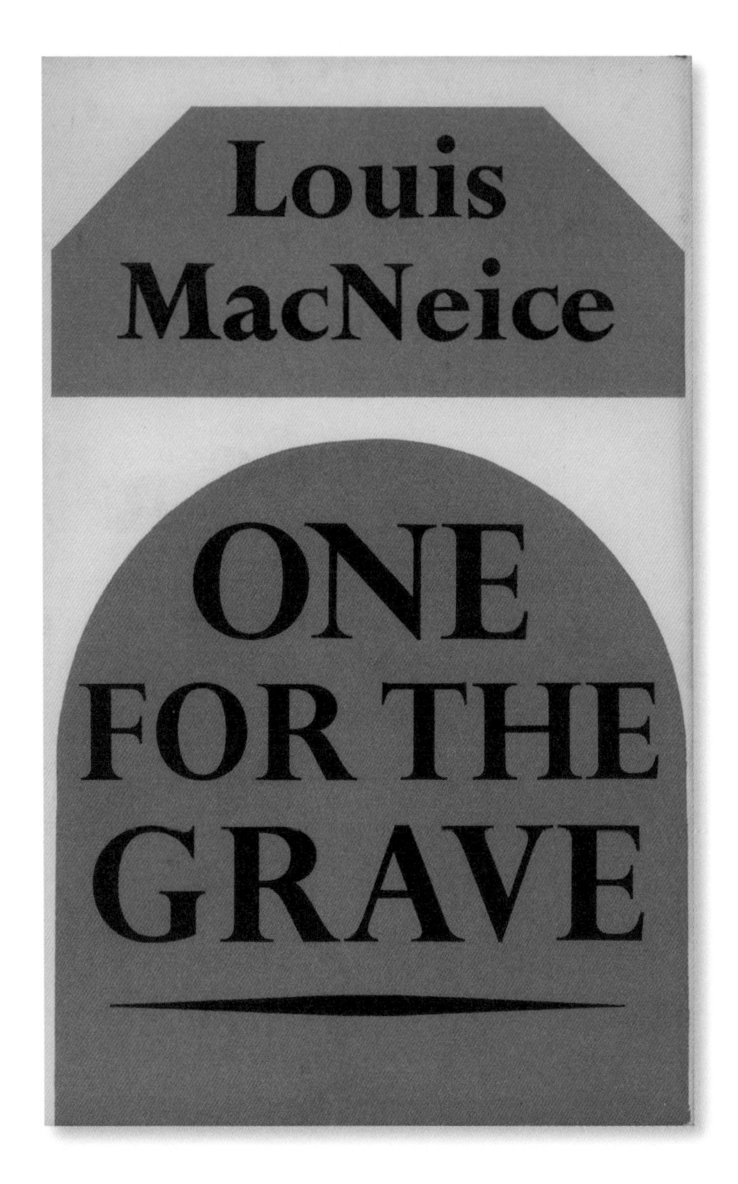
Louis
MacNeice
ONE
FOR THE
GRAVE

31 Monday SUMMER BANK HOLIDAY (UK NOT SCT)

1 Tuesday

2 Wednesday

3 Thursday

4 Friday

5 Saturday

6 Sunday

Autumn Nature Notes

I

The Laburnum top is silent, quite still
In the afternoon yellow September sunlight,
A few leaves yellowing, all its seeds fallen.

Till the goldfinch comes,with a twitching chirrup,
A suddenness, a startlement, at a branch-end.
Then sleek as a lizard, and alert, and abrupt
She enters the thickness, and a machine starts up
Of chitterings, and a tremor of wings, and trillings –
The whole tree trembles and thrills.
It is the engine of her family.
She stokes it full, then flirts out to a branch-end
Showing her barred face identity mask

Then with eerie delicate whistle-chirrup whisperings
She launches away, towards the infinite

And the laburnum subsides to empty.

7 Monday LABOUR DAY (CA)

8 Tuesday

9 Wednesday

10 Thursday

11 Friday

12 Saturday

13 Sunday

A Hummingbird

At Nora's first post-divorce Labor Day bash
there's a fluster and a fuss and a fidget
in the fuschia bells. 'Two fingers of sour mash,
a maraschino cherry.' 'So the digit's
still a unit of measurement?' 'While midgets
continue to demand a slice of the cake.'
'A vibrator, you know, *that* kind of widget.'
Now a ruby-throated hummingbird remakes
itself as it rolls on through mid-forest brake.
'I'm guessing she's had a neck lift *and* lipo.'
'You know I still can't help but think of the *Wake*
as the apogee, you know, of the typo.'
Like an engine rolling on after a crash,
long after whatever it was made a splash.

14 Monday

15 Tuesday

16 Wednesday

17 Thursday

18 Friday

19 Saturday

20 Sunday

Postscript

And some time make the time to drive out west
Into County Clare, along the Flaggy Shore,
In September or October, when the wind
And the light are working off each other
So that the ocean on one side is wild
With foam and glitter, and inland among stones
The surface of a slate-grey lake is lit
By the earthed lightning of a flock of swans,
Their feathers roughed and ruffling, white on white,
Their fully grown headstrong-looking heads
Tucked or cresting or busy underwater.
Useless to think you'll park and capture it
More thoroughly. You are neither here nor there,
A hurry through which known and strange things pass
As big soft buffetings come at the car sideways
And catch the heart off guard and blow it open.

21 Monday

22 Tuesday

23 Wednesday

24 Thursday HERITAGE DAY (ZA)

25 Friday

26 Saturday

27 Sunday

Touch
poems by
THOM
GUNN

28 Monday

29 Tuesday

30 Wednesday

1 Thursday

2 Friday

3 Saturday

4 Sunday

University

On the settling of birds, this man blesses
his daughter.
She'll split fast for Paddington, then slide
east
which may as well be the black beyond
of Calcutta.

The low long curving train opening its
mouth
gulps from his hands her bags to a far-side
seat.
He gawps from his thin-rivered, working
town.

The train roars, the tracks beyond humped
with light.
The rucksack'd man with whom her eyes
meet . . .
Five birds pluck their wings off the train
and fly.

5 Monday

6 Tuesday

7 Wednesday

8 Thursday

9 Friday

10 Saturday

11 Sunday

Les Grands Seigneurs

Men were my buttresses, my castellated towers,
the bowers where I took my rest. The best and worst
of times were men: the peacocks and the cockatoos,
the nightingales, the strutting pink flamingos.

Men were my dolphins, my performing seals; my sailing-ships,
the ballast in my hold. They were the rocking-horses
prancing down the promenade, the bandstand
where the music played. My hurdy-gurdy monkey-men.

I was their queen. I sat enthroned before them,
out of reach. We played at courtly love:
the troubadour, the damsel and the peach.

But after I was wedded, bedded, I became
(yes, overnight) a toy, a plaything, little woman,
wife, a bit of fluff. My husband clicked
his fingers, called my bluff.

12 Monday THANKSGIVING (CA)

13 Tuesday

14 Wednesday

15 Thursday

16 Friday

17 Saturday

18 Sunday

The Second Coming

Turning and turning in the widening gyre
The falcon cannot hear the falconer;
Things fall apart; the centre cannot hold;
Mere anarchy is loosed upon the world,
The blood-dimmed tide is loosed, and everywhere
The ceremony of innocence is drowned;
The best lack all conviction, while the worst
Are full of passionate intensity.

Surely some revelation is at hand;
Surely the Second Coming is at hand.
The Second Coming! Hardly are those words out
When a vast image out of *Spiritus Mundi*
Troubles my sight: somewhere in sands of the desert
A shape with lion body and the head of a man,
A gaze blank and pitiless as the sun,
Is moving its slow thighs, while all about it
Reel shadows of the indignant desert birds.
The darkness drops again; but now I know
That twenty centuries of stony sleep
Were vexed to nightmare by a rocking cradle,
And what rough beast, its hour come round at last,
Slouches towards Bethlehem to be born?

19 Monday

20 Tuesday

21 Wednesday

22 Thursday

23 Friday

24 Saturday

25 Sunday

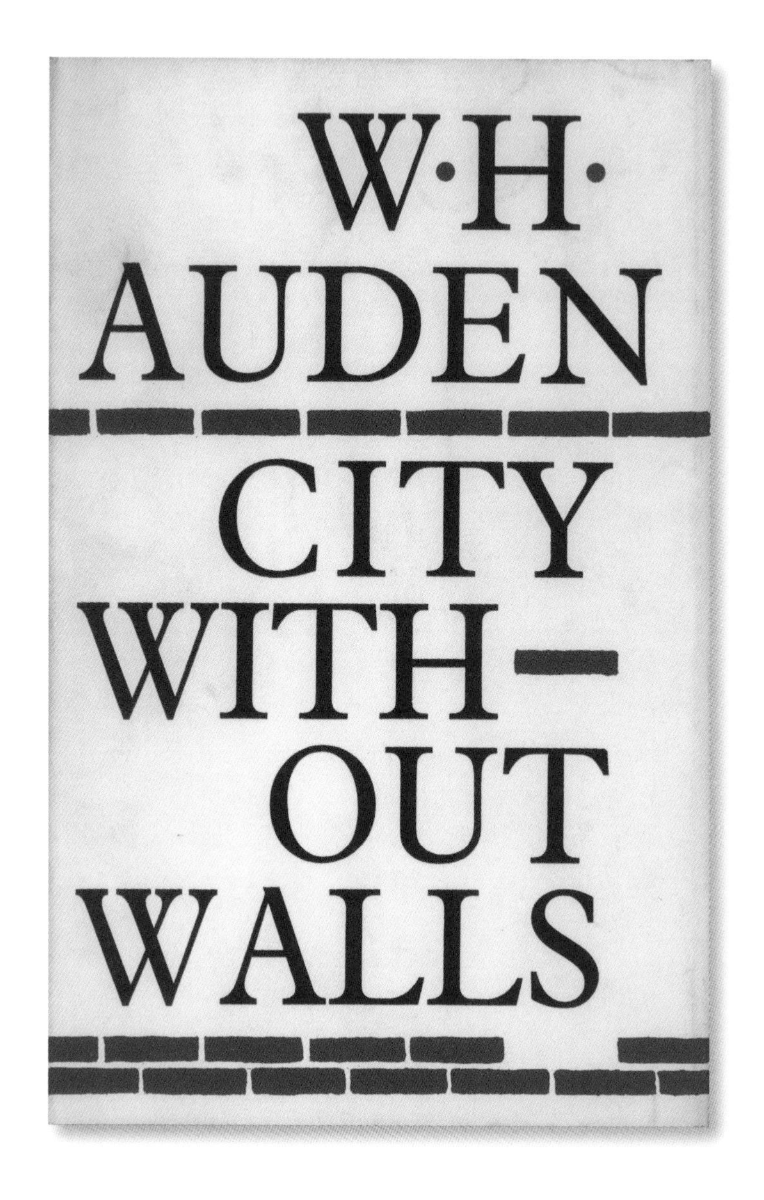
W·H·
AUDEN
CITY
WITH-
OUT
WALLS

26 Monday OCTOBER BANK HOLIDAY (IRL) LABOUR DAY (NZ)

27 Tuesday

28 Wednesday

29 Thursday

30 Friday

31 Saturday

1 Sunday

Stargazer

If I'm not looking at you,
forgive; if I appear
to be scanning the sky,
head thrown back, curious,
ecstatic, shy, strolling
unevenly across the floor
in front of you, my audience,
forgive, and forget what's
happening in my cells.
It's you I'm thinking of
and, voice thrown upwards,
to you I'm speaking, you.

I'm trying to keep this simple
in the time left to me:
luckily, it's a slow
and selective degeneration.
I'm hoping, mainly, to stay present
and straight up despite
the wrong urge that's taken hold,
to say everything, all
at once, to everyone, which
is what I'd like if only
I could stay beyond this moment.

2 Monday

3 Tuesday

4 Wednesday

5 Thursday

6 Friday

7 Saturday

8 Sunday REMEMBRANCE SUNDAY

To Wordsworth

Poet of Nature, thou hast wept to know
That things depart which never may return:
Childhood and youth, friendship and love's first glow,
Have fled like sweet dreams, leaving thee to mourn.
These common woes I feel. One loss is mine
Which thou too feel'st, yet I alone deplore.
Thou wert as a lone star, whose light did shine
On some frail bark in winter's midnight roar:
Thou hast like to a rock-built refuge stood
Above the blind and battling multitude:
In honoured poverty thy voice did weave
Songs consecrate to truth and liberty, –
Deserting these, thou leavest me to grieve,
Thus having been, that thou shouldst cease to be.

9 Monday

10 Tuesday

11 Wednesday

12 Thursday

13 Friday

14 Saturday

15 Sunday

Ancient Music

Winter is icummen in,
Lhude sing Goddamm,
Raineth drop and staineth slop,
And how the wind doth ramm!
            Sing: Goddamm.
Skiddeth bus and sloppeth us,
An ague hath my ham.
Freezeth river, turneth liver,
            Damn you, sing: Goddamm.
Goddamm, Goddamm, 'tis why I am, Goddamm.
            So 'gainst the winter's balm.
Sing goddamm, damm, sing Goddamm.
Sing goddamm, sing goddamm, DAMM.

16 Monday

17 Tuesday

18 Wednesday

19 Thursday

20 Friday

21 Saturday

22 Sunday

He Resigns

Age, and the deaths, and the ghosts.
Her having gone away
in spirit from me. Hosts
of regrets come & find me empty.

I don't feel this will change.
I don't want any thing
or person, familiar or strange.
I don't think I will sing

any more just now,
or ever. I must start
to sit with a blind brow
above an empty heart.

23 Monday

24 Tuesday

25 Wednesday

26 Thursday

27 Friday

28 Saturday

29 Sunday

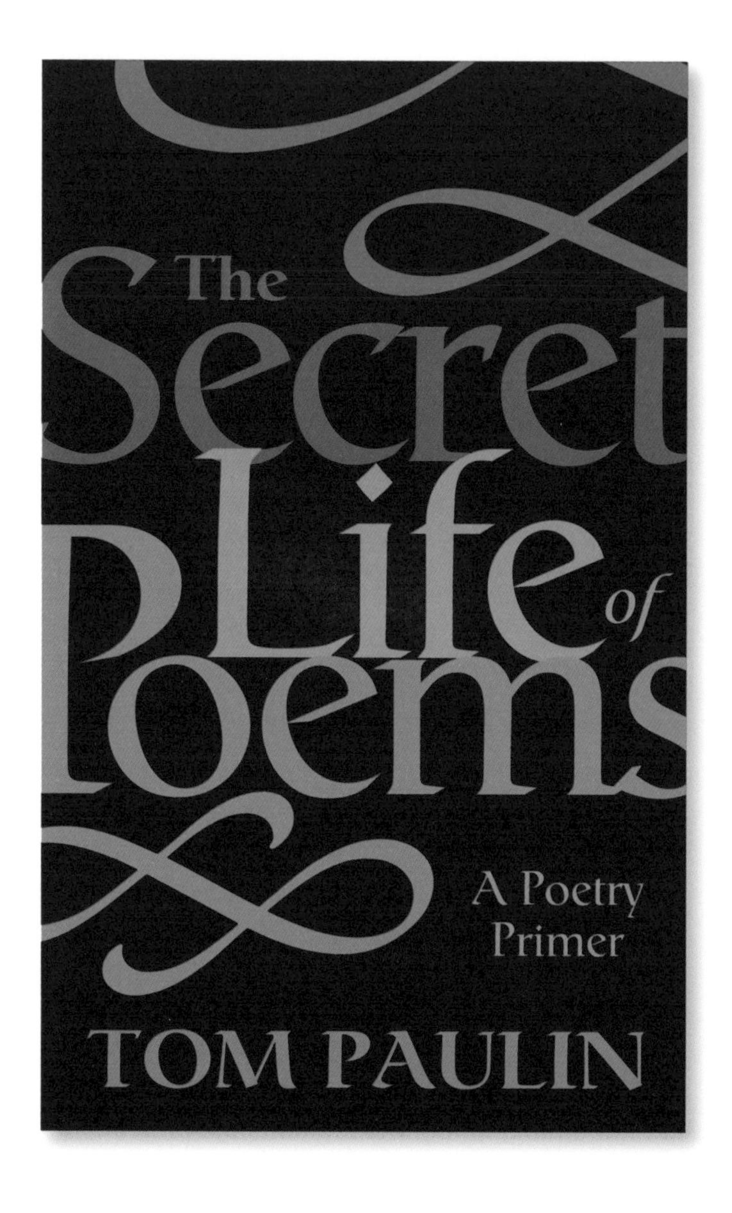
The
Secret
Life
of
Poems
A Poetry
Primer
TOM PAULIN

30 Monday ST ANDREW'S DAY HOLIDAY (SCT)

1 Tuesday

2 Wednesday

3 Thursday

4 Friday

5 Saturday

6 Sunday

When to her lute Corinna sings,
Her voice revives the leaden stringes,
And doth in highest noates appeare
As any challeng'd eccho cleere;
But when she doth of mourning speake,
Ev'n with her sighes the strings do breake.

And, as her lute doth live or die,
Led by her passion, so must I:
For when of pleasure she doth sing,
My thoughts enjoy a sodaine spring;
But if she doth of sorrow speake,
Ev'n from my hart the strings doe breake.

7 Monday

8 Tuesday

9 Wednesday

10 Thursday

11 Friday

12 Saturday

13 Sunday

Scotland's Winter

Now the ice lays its smooth claws on the sill,
The sun looks from the hill
Helmed in his winter casket,
And sweeps his arctic sword across the sky.
The water at the mill
Sounds more hoarse and dull.
The miller's daughter walking by
With frozen fingers soldered to her basket
Seems to be knocking
Upon a hundred leagues of floor
With her light heels, and mocking
Percy and Douglas dead,
And Bruce on his burial bed,
Where he lies white as may
With wars and leprosy,
And all the kings before
This land was kingless,
And all the singers before
This land was songless,
This land that with its dead and living waits the Judgement Day.
But they, the powerless dead,
Listening can hear no more
Than a hard tapping on the sounding floor
A little overhead
Of common heels that do not know
Whence they come or where they go
And are content
With their poor frozen life and shallow banishment.

14 Monday

15 Tuesday

16 Wednesday DAY OF RECONCILIATION (ZA)

17 Thursday

18 Friday

19 Saturday

20 Sunday

Christmas Ornaments

The mice attacked the Holy Family –
The one I bought in Prague, made out of straw.
By Christmas, Joseph was an amputee
And Mary and the baby were no more.
But I have other treasures to display –
Two perching birds, a Santa Claus, a clown,
A rooster from the church in Santa Fé,
A little harp and drum, a shoe, a crown –
Collected in the years I've lived with you,
The years of warmth and love and Christmas trees,
And someone to come home to, someone who
Can share what I bring back from overseas
And sometimes travel with me. Darling, look –
Our moon from Paris, glittering on its hook.

21 Monday

22 Tuesday

23 Wednesday

24 Thursday CHRISTMAS EVE

25 Friday CHRISTMAS DAY (UK, IRL, CA, AUS, ZA, NZ)

26 Saturday BOXING DAY
(UK, CA, AUS, NZ)
DAY OF GOODWILL (ZA)
ST STEPHEN'S DAY (IRL)

27 Sunday

Not Waving but Drowning

Nobody heard him, the dead man,
But still he lay moaning:
I was much further out than you thought
And not waving but drowning.

Poor chap, he always loved larking
And now he's dead
It must have been too cold for him his heart gave way,
They said.

Oh, no no no, it was too cold always
(Still the dead one lay moaning)
I was much too far out all my life
And not waving but drowning.

28 Monday BOXING DAY BANK HOLIDAY (UK, AUS, NZ)

29 Tuesday

30 Wednesday

31 Thursday NEW YEAR'S EVE

1 Friday NEW YEAR'S DAY (UK, IRL, CA, AUS, ZA, NZ)

2 Saturday NEW YEAR HOLIDAY (SCT) DAY AFTER NEW YEAR'S DAY (NZ)

3 Sunday

A Brief Chronology of Faber's Poetry Publishing

1925 Geoffrey Faber acquires an interest in The Scientific Press and renames the firm Faber and Gwyer. ¶ The poet/bank clerk T. S. Eliot is recruited. 'What will impress my directors favourably is the sense that in you we have found a man who combines literary gifts with business instincts.' – Geoffrey Faber to T. S. Eliot ¶ Eliot brought with him *The Criterion*, the quarterly periodical he had been editing since 1922. (*The Waste Land* had appeared in its first issue, brilliantly establishing its reputation.) He continued to edit it from the Faber offices until it closed in 1939. Though unprofitable it was hugely influential, introducing early work by Auden, Empson and Spender, amongst others, and promoting many notable European writers, including Proust and Valéry. ¶ Publication of T. S. Eliot's *Poems, 1909–1925*, which included *The Waste Land* and a new sequence, *The Hollow Men*. ¶

1927 From 1927 to 1931 Faber publishes a series of illustrated pamphlets known as *The Ariel Poems* containing unpublished poems by an eminent poet (Thomas Hardy, W. B. Yeats, Harold Monro, Edith Sitwell and Edmund Blunden to name but a few) along with an illustration, usually in colour, by a leading contemporary artist (including Eric Gill, Eric Ravilious, Paul Nash and Graham Sutherland). ¶

1928 Faber and Gwyer announce the *Selected Poems of Ezra Pound*, with an introduction and notes by Eliot. ¶

1929 Geoffrey Faber buys out Lady Gwyer and oversees the birth of the Faber and Faber imprint. Legend has it that Walter de la Mare, the father of Faber director Richard de la Mare, suggested the euphonious repetition: another Faber in the company name 'because you can't have too much of a good thing'. ¶

1930 W. H. Auden becomes a Faber poet with a collection entitled simply *Poems*. ¶ Eliot publishes *Ash Wednesday*. ¶

1933 Stephen Spender becomes a Faber poet with his first collection *Poems*, a companion piece to Auden's 1930 work of the same name. ¶ The first British edition of James Joyce's *Pomes Penyeach* is published. ¶

1935 The American poet Marianne Moore publishes with Faber. 'Miss Moore's poems form part of a small body of durable poetry written in our time.' – T. S. Eliot ¶ Louis MacNeice becomes a Faber poet. 'The most original Irish poet of his generation.' – Faber catalogue 1935 ¶

1936 The hugely influential *Faber Book of Modern Verse* (edited by Michael Roberts) is published. ¶

1937 *In Parenthesis* by David Jones is published. 'This is an epic of war. But it is like no other war-book because for the first time that experience has been reduced to "a shape in words." The impression still remains that this book is one of the most remarkable literary achievements of our time.' – *Times Literary Supplement* ¶ W. H. Auden is awarded the Queen's Gold Medal for Poetry. ¶

1939 T. S. Eliot's *Old Possum's Book of Practical Cats* is published with a book jacket illustrated by the author. Originally called *Pollicle Dogs and Jellicle Cats*, the poems were written for his five godchildren. The eldest of these was Geoffrey Faber's son Tom – himself much later a director of Faber and Faber. ¶

1944 Walter de la Mare's *Peacock Pie* is published with illustrations by Edward Ardizzone. ¶ Philip Larkin's first novel, *A Girl in Winter*, is published. 'A young man with an exceptionally clear sense of what, as a writer, he means to do.' – *Times Literary Supplement* ¶

1948 T. S. Eliot wins the Nobel Prize in Literature. ¶

1949 Ezra Pound's *Pisan Cantos* is published. 'The most incomprehensible passages are often more stimulating than much comprehensibility which passes for poetry today.' – *Times Literary Supplement* ¶

1954 *The Ariel Poems* are revived with a new set of pamphlets by W. H. Auden, Stephen Spender, Louis MacNeice, T. S. Eliot, Walter de la Mare, Cecil Day Lewis and Roy Campbell. The artists include Edward Ardizzone, Edward Bawden, Michael Ayrton and John Piper. ¶

1957 Ted Hughes comes to Faber with *The Hawk in the Rain*. ¶ Siegfried Sassoon receives the Queen's Gold Medal for Poetry. ¶

1959 Robert Lowell's collection *Life Studies* is published. ¶

1960 Saint-John Perse wins the Nobel Prize in Literature.

1961 Geoffrey Faber dies. ¶ Ted Hughes's first collection of children's poems, *Meet My Folks*, is published. ¶

1963 Sylvia Plath's novel *The Bell Jar* is published by Faber in the year of her death. ¶ The Geoffrey Faber Memorial Prize is established as an annual prize awarded in alternating years to a single volume of poetry or fiction by a Commonwealth author under forty. ¶

1964 Philip Larkin's *The Whitsun Weddings* is published. ¶

1965 T. S. Eliot dies. ¶ Sylvia Plath's posthumous collection, *Ariel*, is published. 'Her extraordinary achievement, poised as she was between volatile emotional state and the edge of the precipice.' – Frieda Hughes ¶ Philip Larkin is awarded the Queen's Gold Medal for Poetry. ¶

1966 Seamus Heaney comes to Faber with *Death of a Naturalist*. ¶

1968 Ted Hughes's *The Iron Man* is published. ¶

1971 Stephen Spender is awarded the Queen's Gold Medal for Poetry. ¶

1973 Paul Muldoon comes to Faber with his first collection, *New Weather*. ¶

1974 Ted Hughes receives the Queen's Gold Medal for Poetry. ¶

1977 Tom Paulin comes to Faber with his first collection, *A State of Justice*. ¶ Norman Nicholson receives the Queen's Gold Medal for Poetry. ¶

1980 Csezlaw Milosz wins the Nobel Prize in Literature. ¶

1981 *Cats*, the Andrew Lloyd-Webber musical based on *Old Possum's Book of Practical Cats,* opens in London. ¶

1984 *Rich*, a collection by Faber's own poetry editor, Craig Raine, is published. 'Puts us in touch with life as unexpectedly and joyfully as early Pasternak.' – John Bayley ¶ Ted Hughes becomes Poet Laureate. ¶

1985 Douglas Dunn's collection *Elegies* is the Whitbread Book of the Year. ¶

1986 Vikram Seth's *The Golden Gate* is published. ¶

1987 Seamus Heaney's *The Haw Lantern* wins the Whitbread Prize for Poetry. ¶

1988 Derek Walcott is awarded the Queen's Gold Medal for Poetry. ¶

1992 Derek Walcott wins the Nobel Prize in Literature. ¶ Thom Gunn's collection *The Man with the Night Sweats* wins the Forward Poetry Prize for Best Collection, while Simon Armitage's *Kid* wins Best First Collection. ¶

1993 Andrew Motion wins the Whitbread Prize for Biography for his book on Philip Larkin. ¶ Don Paterson's *Nil Nil* wins the Forward Poetry Prize for Best First Collection. ¶

1994 Paul Muldoon wins the T. S. Eliot Prize for *The Annals of Chile*. ¶ Alice Oswald wins an Eric Gregory Award. ¶

1995 Seamus Heaney wins the Nobel Prize in Literature. ¶

1996 Wislawa Szymborska wins the Nobel Prize in Literature. ¶ Seamus Heaney's *The Spirit Level* wins the Whitbread Prize for Poetry. 'Touched by a sense of wonder.' – Blake Morrison ¶

1997 Don Paterson wins the T. S. Eliot Prize for *God's Gift to Women* ¶ Lavinia Greenlaw wins the Forward Prize for Best Single Poem for 'A World Where News Travelled Slowly'. ¶ Ted Hughes's *Tales from Ovid* is the Whitbread Book of the Year. 'A breathtaking book.' – John Carey ¶

1998 Ted Hughes wins the Whitbread Book of the Year for the second time running with *Birthday Letters*, which also wins the T. S. Eliot Prize. 'Language like lava, its molten turmoils hardening into jagged shapes.' – John Carey ¶ Ted Hughes is awarded the Order of Merit. ¶ Christopher Logue receives the Wilfred Owen Poetry Award. ¶

1999 Seamus Heaney's *Beowulf* wins the Whitbread Book of the Year Award. '[Heaney is the] one living poet who can rightly claim to be Beowulf's heir.' – *New York Times* ¶ A memorial service for Ted Hughes is held at Westminster Abbey. In his speech Seamus Heaney calls Hughes 'a guardian spirit of the land and language'. ¶ Hugo Williams wins the T. S. Eliot Prize for his collection *Billy's Rain*. ¶ Andrew Motion is appointed Poet Laureate. ¶

2000 Seamus Heaney receives the Wilfred Owen Poetry Award. ¶

2002 Alice Oswald wins the T. S. Eliot Prize for Poetry for her collection *Dart*. ¶

2003 Paul Muldoon is awarded the Pulitzer Prize for Poetry for *Moy Sand and Gravel*. ¶

2004 August Kleinzahler receives the International Griffin Prize for *The Strange Hours Travellers Keep*. ¶ Hugo Williams is awarded the Queen's Gold Medal for Poetry. ¶

2005 David Harsent wins the Forward Prize for Best Collection for *Legion*. ¶ Harold Pinter receives the Wilfred Owen Poetry Award. ¶ Charles Simic receives the International Griffin Prize for *Selected Poems 1963–2003*. ¶ Nick Laird wins an Eric Gregory Award. ¶

2006 Christopher Logue wins the Whitbread Prize for Poetry for *Cold Calls*. ¶ The Geoffrey Faber Memorial Prize is awarded to Alice Oswald for *Woods Etc*. ¶ Seamus Heaney wins the T. S. Eliot Prize for *District and Circle*. ¶

2007 Tony Harrison is awarded the Wilfred Owen Award for Poetry. ¶ Daljit Nagra wins the Forward Prize for Best first Collection for *Look We Have Coming to Dover!* ¶ James Fenton receives the Queen's Gold Medal for Poetry. ¶

2008 Daljit Nagra wins the South Bank Show / Arts Council Decibel Award. ¶ Mick Imlah's collection *The Lost Leader* wins the Forward Prize for Best Collection. ¶

2009 Carol Ann Duffy becomes Poet Laureate. ¶ Don Paterson's *Rain* wins the Forward Poetry Prize for Best Collection while *The Striped World* by Emma Jones wins the Best First Collection Prize. ¶

2010 *The Song of Lunch* by Christopher Reid is shortlisted for the Ted Hughes Award for New Work in Poetry and he is awarded the Costa Book Prize for *A Scattering.* ¶ The John Florio Prize for Italian Translation 2010 is awarded to Jamie McKendrick for *The Embrace.* ¶ Derek Walcott wins both the Warwick Prize and the T. S. Eliot Prize for Poetry for his collection *White Egrets.* ¶ *Rain* by Don Paterson is shortlisted for the Saltire Scottish Book of the Year. ¶ Tony Harrison is awarded the Prix Européen de Litérature. ¶ The Keats–Shelley Prize is awarded to Simon Armitage for his poem *The Present.* ¶ The Forward Prize for Best Collection is awarded to Seamus Heaney for *Human Chain.* ¶ Also shortlisted for the Forward Prize for Best Collection are Lachlan Mackinnon for *Small Hours* and Jo Shapcott for *Of Mutability.* ¶ The Centre for Literacy in Primary Education (CLPE) Poetry Prize is awarded to Carol Ann Duffy for *New and Collected Poems for Children.* ¶ Alice Oswald wins the Ted Hughes Award for New Work in Poetry for *Weeds and Wild Flowers.* ¶ *The Striped World* by Emma Jones is shortlisted for the Adelaide Festival Poetry Award. ¶ The Queen's Medal for Poetry is awarded to Don Paterson. ¶

2011 *Of Mutability* by Jo Shapcott is the Costa Book of the Year. ¶ *Human Chain* by Seamus Heaney and *Maggot* by Paul Muldoon are both shortlisted for the *Irish Times* Poetry Now Award. ¶ *Night* by David Harsent is shortlisted for the Forward Prize for Best Collection. ¶ 'Bees' by Jo Shapcott is shortlisted for the Forward Prize for Best Poem. ¶ A new digital edition of T. S. Eliot's *The Waste Land* for iPad is launched, bringing to life one of the most revolutionary poems of the last hundred years, illuminated by a wealth of interactive features. ¶ The Queen's Gold Medal for Poetry is awarded to Jo Shapcott. ¶ At Westminster Abbey a memorial is dedicated to Ted Hughes in Poets' Corner. ¶

2012 *The Death of King Arthur* by Simon Armitage is shortlisted for the T. S. Eliot Prize. ¶ *The World's Two Smallest Humans* by Julia Copus is shortlisted for the T. S. Eliot Prize and the Costa Book Award. ¶ David Harsent's collection *Night* wins the 2012 International Griffin Poetry Prize. ¶ *81 Austerities* by Sam Riviere wins the Felix Dennis Prize for Best First Collection, one of the Forward Prizes for Poetry. ¶ *Farmers Cross* by Bernard O'Donoghue is shortlisted for the Irish Times Poetry Now Award. ¶

2013 The Forward Prize for Best First Collection is awarded to Emily Berry for *Dear Boy* ¶ Hugo Williams is shortlisted for the Forward Prize for Best Single

Poem for 'From the Dialysis Ward' ¶
Alice Oswald is awarded the Warwick Prize for Writing for her collection *Memorial*, which also wins the Poetry Society's Corneliu M. Popescu Prize for poetry in translation. ¶

In his eulogy for Seamus Heaney, Paul Muldoon says, 'We remember the beauty of Seamus Heaney – as a bard, and in his being.' In November the first official tribute evenings to Heaney are held at Harvard, then in New York, followed by events at the Royal Festival Hall in London, the Waterfront Hall, Belfast, and the Sheldonian, Oxford. ¶

Acknowledgements

Poetry

All poetry reprinted by permission of Faber & Faber unless otherwise stated.

'Poetry' taken from *Tyrannosaurus Rex versus the Corduroy Kid* © Simon Armitage ¶ 'The Sphinx', copyright © 1939 and renewed 1967 by W.H. Auden and Christopher Isherwood; from *W. H. Auden Collected Poems* by W. H. Auden. Used by permission of Curtis Brown, Ltd. and Random House, an imprint and division of Random House LLC and All rights reserved. Any third party use of this material, outside of this publication, is prohibited. Interested parties must apply directly to Random House LLC for permission. ¶ 'He Resigns' taken from *Collected Poems* © Estate of John Berryman by permission of Faber & Faber and Farrar, Straus and Giroux, LLC. ¶ 'The Licorice fields at Pontefract' taken from *Collected Poems* by John Betjeman © Estate of John Betjeman 1955, 1958, 1962, 1964, 1968, 1970, 1979, 1981, 1982, 2001. Reproduced by permission of John Murray, an imprint of Hodder and Stoughton Ltd. ¶ 'Christmas Ornaments' taken from *Family Values* © Wendy Cope ¶ 'Silver' taken from *Selected Poems,* reprinted by permission of The Literary Trustees of Walter de la Mare and The Society of Authors as their Representative ¶ 'Seferis' taken from *Selected Poems* © Estate of Lawrence Durrell ¶ 'Preludes IV' taken from *The Complete Poems & Plays* © Estate of T. S. Eliot ¶ 'After Africa' taken from *Six Children* © Mark Ford ¶ 'Streetlamps' taken from *Muscovy* © Matthew Francis ¶ 'Coleridge' taken from *The Casual Perfect* © Lavinia Greenlaw ¶ 'The Long Walk to the End of the Garden' taken from *Night* © David Harsent ¶ 'Postscript' taken from *The Spirit Level* © Estate of Seamus Heaney ¶ 'Autumn Nature Notes I' taken from *Collected Poems* © Estate of Ted Hughes ¶ 'Window' taken from *The Striped World* © Emma Jones ¶ 'Epithalamium' taken from *Go Giants* © Nick Laird ¶ 'Forget What Did' taken from *The Complete Poems* © Estate of Philip Larkin ¶ 'Les Grands Seigneurs' taken from *Hare Soup* © Estate of Dorothy Molloy ¶ 'Holy Island' taken from *The Customs House* © Andrew Motion 'Scotland's Winter' taken from *Collected Poems* © Estate of Edwin Muir ¶ 'A Hummingbird' taken from *Maggot* © Paul Muldoon by permission of Faber & Faber and Farrar, Straus and Giroux, LLC. ¶ 'University' taken from *Look We Have Coming To Dover!* © Daljit Nagra ¶ 'field' taken from *Woods Etc.* © Alice Oswald ¶ 'Poetry' taken from *Selected Poems* © Don Paterson 2012. Reproduced by permission of the author c/o Rogers, Coleridge & White Ltd, 20 Powis Mews, London W11 1JN ¶ 'Mirror' taken from *Collected Poems* © Estate of Sylvia Plath ¶ 'Ancient Music' by Ezra Pound from *Personae* © 1926 by Ezra Pound. Reprinted by permission of New Directions Publishing Corp. ¶ 'Espresso' taken from *Nonsense* © Christopher Reid 2012. Reproduced by permission of the author c/o Rogers, Coleridge & White Ltd, 20 Powis Mews, London W11 1JN ¶ 'Stargazer' taken from *Of Mutability* © Jo Shapcott ¶ 'Not Waving But Drowning' by Stevie Smith from *Collected Poems of Stevie Smith* © 1957 by Stevie Smith. Reprinted by permission of New Directions Publishing Corp and Estate of Stevie Smith. ¶ 'In My Craft or Sullen Art' by Dylan Thomas taken from *Centenary Collection* © Estate of Dylan Thomas. ¶ 'Love after Love' taken from *Collected Poems* © Derek Walcott by permission of Faber & Faber and Farrar, Straus and Giroux, LLC.

Picture Credits

All jacket designs by Berthold Wolpe except for *The Secret Life of Poems*, which is by Alex Kirby, and *The Faber Book of Nonsense Verse*, designed by Faber and Faber Ltd, with illustrations by Edward Lear.

NOTES

NOTES

NOTES

NOTES

NOTES

NOTES

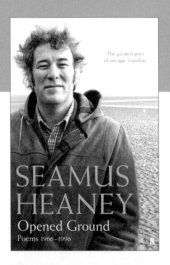

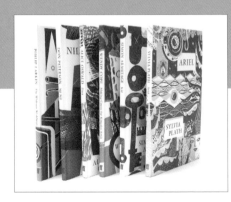

Charles Boyle
The Age of Cardboard and String

Eiléan Ní Chuilleanáin
Selected Poems

Amy Clampitt
Collected Poems

Douglas Dunn
New Selected Poems 1964–1999

Robert Henryson
The Testament of Cresseid & Seven Fables
Translated by Seamus Heaney

Michael Hofmann
Selected Poems

Mick Imlah
The Lost Leader

August Kleinzahler
Sleeping It Off in Rapid City
New and Selected Poems

Jamie McKendrick
Ink Stone

Dorothy Molloy
Gethsemane Day

Dorothy Molloy
Hare Soup

Marianne Moore
Complete Poems

Tom Paulin
The Road to Inver

Maurice Riordan
The Holy Land

Frederick Seidel
Selected Poems

Charles Simic
Selected Poems 1963–2003